OLIVER KAIN

Discovering Dallas - A Guide to the Top 10 Must-See Attractions

Contents

1

Dallas, Texas

"Discovering Dallas: A Guide to the Top 10 Must-See Attractions"

Dallas, Texas is one of the most vibrant and exciting cities in the United

States. Whether you are a first-time visitor or a seasoned traveler, this city offers something for everyone. From its rich cultural heritage to its exciting entertainment scene, Dallas is a destination that is not to be missed. In this book, we will explore some of the reasons why you should consider visiting Dallas on your next vacation.

One of the most striking things about Dallas is its rich history. The city was founded in 1841 and has a long and fascinating story to tell. From the days of the Old West, to the rise of the oil industry and the modern metropolis that we see today, Dallas has always been a city of change and growth. Visitors can experience this rich history by visiting places like the Sixth Floor Museum at Dealey Plaza, which details the events of the assassination of President John F. Kennedy, or the Pioneer Plaza, which pays homage to the city's Western heritage.

Another reason why you should visit Dallas is for its exciting entertainment scene. The city is home to a variety of world-class entertainment venues, from the American Airlines Center, which is home to the Dallas Mavericks and the Dallas Stars, to the AT&T Stadium, the home of the Dallas Cowboys. Dallas is also home to numerous performing arts venues, including the Winspear Opera House and the Majestic Theater, which regularly host productions from some of the country's leading companies.

For those who are interested in exploring the city's cultural side, Dallas is also home to a number of fantastic museums and art galleries. The Dallas Museum of Art is one of the largest and most comprehensive art museums in the country, with a collection that spans thousands of years and many different cultures. Visitors can also explore the collection of the Nasher Sculpture Center, which showcases works by some of the world's most famous sculptors.

In addition to its cultural offerings, Dallas is also a great place to experience some of the best shopping, dining, and nightlife in the country. The city is home to a number of shopping destinations, including the Galleria Dallas, one of the largest malls in the country, and the Bishop Arts District, which is known for its unique boutiques and shops. Dallas is also a food lover's paradise, with a range of dining options that range from casual cafes and bistros to upscale restaurants and high-end steakhouses.

For those who are looking for an outdoor experience, Dallas is also home to a number of parks and green spaces that offer opportunities for hiking, biking, and other outdoor activities. The city is also home to a number of lakes and rivers, making it a popular destination for boating, fishing, and other water-based activities.

One of the most exciting things about Dallas is its close proximity to other great destinations. Whether you're looking to explore the beautiful countryside of Texas, or you're interested in visiting other major cities in the region, Dallas is a great starting point. The city is located just a short drive from Fort Worth, which is home to the Fort Worth Stockyards, as well as Austin, the state capital of Texas.

In conclusion, Dallas is a city that is rich in history, culture, and excitement. Whether you're interested in exploring its museums and galleries, experiencing its world-class entertainment scene, or simply enjoying its great outdoors, Dallas is a destination that should not be missed. So, why not plan your next vacation to Dallas, Texas and discover all that this vibrant city has to offer.

2

Chapter 2

Top 10 Most Popular Tourist Spots in Dallas, Texas

3

Chapter 3

Dealey Plaza and the John F. Kennedy Memorial

Dealey Plaza and the John F. Kennedy Memorial in Dallas, Texas, are two popular tourist spots that are deeply connected to one of the most historic events in American history – the assassination of President John F. Kennedy. These two landmarks offer visitors a unique opportunity to reflect on the legacy of the former President, while also learning more about the events that took place on November 22, 1963.

Dealey Plaza is a city park located in the heart of Dallas, and it is widely recognized as the site of Kennedy's assassination. The plaza is surrounded by several historic buildings, including the Texas School Book Depository, from where Lee Harvey Oswald is believed to have fired the shots that killed Kennedy. Visitors can walk along the grassy knoll and stand on the exact spot where Kennedy was shot.

The John F. Kennedy Memorial, located a few blocks away from Dealey Plaza, serves as a tribute to the fallen President. The memorial is a simple, yet powerful, structure that was designed to symbolize the loss of Kennedy and the spirit of the American people. The memorial consists of a square, concrete structure that is surrounded by a ring of tall concrete columns. The columns symbolize the collective strength of the American people, while the open center represents the void left by Kennedy's passing.

Visiting Dealey Plaza and the John F. Kennedy Memorial is a must for anyone who wants to understand the events that took place in Dallas on November 22, 1963. Whether you are a history buff, a student of politics, or simply a curious tourist, these two landmarks offer a wealth of information about one of the most significant events in American history. Visitors can learn about Kennedy's presidency, his accomplishments, and his vision for the country, as well as the events leading up to his assassination and its aftermath.

In addition to learning about the historical significance of these two landmarks, visiting Dealey Plaza and the John F. Kennedy Memorial is also a great way to pay homage to a beloved former President. Kennedy is widely regarded as one of the most charismatic and inspirational leaders in American history, and his legacy continues to inspire people around the world. By visiting these two landmarks, visitors can pay their respects to Kennedy and gain a deeper understanding of his life, legacy, and impact on the world.

Finally, visiting Dealey Plaza and the John F. Kennedy Memorial is a unique opportunity to reflect on the tragedy of November 22, 1963. These two landmarks serve as a reminder of the fragility of life and the importance of cherishing every moment. They offer a quiet, peaceful, and contemplative space for visitors to reflect on their own lives and to remember the sacrifices that Kennedy made on behalf of his country.

In conclusion, Dealey Plaza and the John F. Kennedy Memorial in Dallas, Texas, are two must-visit landmarks for anyone interested in history, politics, or simply paying homage to a beloved former President. These two landmarks offer a wealth of information about the events of November 22, 1963, as well as a unique opportunity to reflect on Kennedy's life, legacy, and impact on the world. Whether you are a history buff, a student of politics, or simply a curious tourist, Dealey Plaza and the John F. Kennedy Memorial are two landmarks that should be at the top of your list of things to see in Dallas.

4

Chapter 4

The Sixth Floor Museum at Dealey Plaza

The Sixth Floor Museum at Dealey Plaza in Dallas, Texas, is a must-visit destination for anyone interested in the life and legacy of President John F. Kennedy. This museum, located on the sixth floor of the former Texas School Book Depository building, offers visitors an in-depth look at the events of November 22, 1963, when Kennedy was assassinated in Dallas.

The museum is a well-curated, interactive, and educational experience that tells the story of Kennedy's presidency, his impact on the world, and the events leading up to his assassination. Visitors can learn about Kennedy's life and his political vision, as well as his work on civil rights, space exploration, and international relations. The museum also provides an in-depth look at the events of November 22, 1963, and the investigations that followed, including the Warren Commission Report and the findings of the House Select Committee on Assassinations.

One of the highlights of the museum is the "Dealey Plaza" exhibit, which provides an interactive simulation of the assassination. Visitors can stand on the exact spot where Kennedy was shot and learn about the various theories surrounding the assassination. The museum also features a comprehensive collection of artifacts, including original film footage, photographs, documents, and personal belongings that help bring the events of November 22, 1963, to life.

In addition to its educational value, the Sixth Floor Museum is also a powerful tribute to Kennedy's legacy. Kennedy is widely regarded as one of the most inspiring leaders in American history, and his impact on the world continues to be felt today. The museum offers visitors a unique opportunity to learn about Kennedy's life, his vision for the country, and his impact on the world, as well as to pay homage to his memory.

Visiting the Sixth Floor Museum is also a great way to gain a deeper understanding of one of the most significant events in American history. Whether you are a history buff, a student of politics, or simply a curious tourist, this museum offers a wealth of information about the life and legacy of Kennedy, as well as the events that took place on November 22, 1963. Visitors can gain a better understanding of the political, social, and cultural context of the time, as well as the impact that the assassination had on the country and the world.

Finally, visiting the Sixth Floor Museum is a unique opportunity to reflect on the tragedy of November 22, 1963. This museum serves as a reminder of the fragility of life and the importance of cherishing every moment. It offers visitors a quiet, peaceful, and contemplative space to reflect on their own lives and to remember the sacrifices that Kennedy made on behalf of his country.

In conclusion, The Sixth Floor Museum at Dealey Plaza in Dallas, Texas, is a must-visit destination for anyone interested in the life and legacy of President John F. Kennedy. This museum offers a well-curated, interactive, and educational experience that tells the story of Kennedy's presidency, his impact on the world, and the events leading up to his assassination. Whether you are a history buff, a student of politics, or simply a curious tourist, the Sixth Floor Museum is a landmark that should be at the top of your list of things to see in Dallas.

5

Chapter 5

AT&T Stadium (Home of the Dallas Cowboys)

AT&T Stadium, located in Arlington, Texas, is the home of the Dallas

Cowboys, one of the most successful and recognizable NFL teams. The stadium has been a staple of the Dallas community since it opened in 2009, and it offers a unique and exciting experience for fans and visitors alike. Whether you're a Cowboys fan or just looking for a fun day out, there are several reasons why you should visit AT&T Stadium.

First and foremost, AT&T Stadium is a marvel of modern engineering and design. The stadium boasts a retractable roof, which can be opened or closed depending on the weather. This feature alone makes it worth a visit, as it offers a unique experience compared to other NFL stadiums. Additionally, the stadium has a giant video board that measures 72 feet high by 160 feet wide, making it one of the largest video boards in the world. This board provides an immersive experience for fans and helps to create a true home field advantage for the Cowboys.

Another reason to visit AT&T Stadium is the sheer size of the facility. The stadium has a seating capacity of over 80,000, making it one of the largest NFL stadiums in the country. The large size of the stadium means that there are plenty of seating options available, from luxury suites to general admission seating, so there is something for everyone. The large size also means that there is plenty of room for food and drink concessions, merchandise stands, and other amenities.

The Cowboys themselves are also a big draw for visitors. The team has a rich history and has won five Super Bowl championships, making it one of the most successful NFL franchises of all time. With a roster of talented players and a passionate fan base, the Cowboys always bring excitement and energy to AT&T Stadium on game day. Attending a game at AT&T Stadium is a truly unique experience that is not to be missed.

Beyond the actual games, AT&T Stadium also offers a variety of other events and activities. The stadium has hosted concerts from some of the biggest names in music, including Taylor Swift, George Strait, and Beyonce. The facility also hosts other events such as monster truck rallies and college football games. These events offer a fun and exciting way to experience AT&T Stadium even if you're not a Cowboys fan.

Finally, AT&T Stadium is located in the Dallas-Fort Worth Metroplex, one of the largest and most vibrant metropolitan areas in the United States. The area is home to numerous other attractions, including Six Flags Over Texas, the Fort Worth Stockyards, and the AT&T Stadium itself. The area also offers a variety of dining and entertainment options, making it a great destination for a weekend getaway.

In conclusion, there are many reasons why you should visit AT&T Stadium in Arlington, Texas. From the impressive design and engineering to the talented Cowboys team and the other events and activities offered, AT&T Stadium is a truly unique and exciting experience that should not be missed. Whether you're a die-hard Cowboys fan or just looking for a fun day out, AT&T Stadium is a must-visit destination.

6

Chapter 6

The Dallas Arboretum and Botanical Garden

The Dallas Arboretum and Botanical Garden is a 66-acre public garden located on the southeastern shore of White Rock Lake in Dallas, Texas. This stunning park is a hidden gem that offers a tranquil escape from the bustling city and provides visitors with an opportunity to connect with nature and experience the beauty of the outdoors. If you're looking for a peaceful and relaxing day out, then the Dallas Arboretum is the perfect destination for you.

One of the reasons why you should visit the Dallas Arboretum is its stunning gardens and landscapes. The park boasts a diverse collection of plants and flowers, ranging from exotic species to native Texas wildflowers. The garden's landscapes are carefully curated to create a harmonious and breathtaking display of color and form, with seasonal plantings that change throughout the year. Visitors can stroll through the gardens, admire the blooming flowers, and take in the beauty of the surrounding scenery.

Another reason to visit the Dallas Arboretum is its rich history and cultural significance. The garden was founded in 1984, and since then it has become a vital part of the Dallas community. The park is also home to several historic structures, including the historic DeGolyer House, which serves as the main entrance to the park and houses several exhibitions and events.

The park also offers a variety of educational opportunities, with classes and workshops available for both adults and children. These classes and workshops range from gardening and horticulture to photography and bird watching. The Dallas Arboretum is dedicated to educating visitors about the importance of plants and wildlife, and the park's knowledgeable staff and volunteers are always on hand to answer questions and provide information.

In addition to its stunning gardens and educational opportunities, the Dallas Arboretum also offers a range of recreational activities for visitors to enjoy. The park has several hiking and biking trails that wind through its lush landscapes, providing visitors with a chance to get some exercise and enjoy the fresh air. The park also offers picnic areas, a playground, and several lakes and ponds, making it the perfect destination for a family outing.

The park is also a popular venue for events and weddings, and its stunning scenery and historic buildings make it the perfect backdrop for any special occasion. Whether you're looking to host a large event or a small, intimate gathering, the Dallas Arboretum has the perfect space for you.

Finally, the Dallas Arboretum is located in a beautiful and convenient location, just a short drive from downtown Dallas. The park is surrounded by several other attractions, including the Dallas World Aquarium, the Perot Museum of Nature and Science, and the Dallas Zoo, making it a great destination for a day trip.

In conclusion, the Dallas Arboretum and Botanical Garden is a must-visit destination for anyone looking to experience the beauty of nature and escape the hustle and bustle of the city. With its stunning gardens, rich history, and educational opportunities, the park offers something for everyone. Whether you're a seasoned gardener or just looking for a relaxing day out, the Dallas Arboretum is the perfect destination for you.

7

Chapter 7

The Perot Museum of Nature and Science

The Perot Museum of Nature and Science is a world-class museum located in Dallas, Texas that offers a unique and interactive learning experience for visitors of all ages. The museum is dedicated to inspiring and educating people about the wonders of science and the natural world, and it provides a dynamic and engaging platform for exploring the mysteries of our planet and beyond. If you're looking for a fun, educational, and truly memorable day out, then the Perot Museum is the perfect destination for you.

One of the reasons why you should visit the Perot Museum is its state-of-the-art exhibits. The museum features 11 permanent exhibits that cover a wide range of subjects, including the natural sciences, earth sciences, paleontology, health, and technology. The exhibits are designed to be both educational and entertaining, with interactive displays and hands-on activities that allow visitors to experience the thrill of discovery for themselves.

Another reason to visit the Perot Museum is its commitment to science education. The museum is dedicated to inspiring the next generation of scientists and engineers, and it offers a variety of educational programs and classes for students of all ages. Whether you're a young learner or an adult, you'll find something of interest at the Perot Museum, with classes and workshops covering subjects such as robotics, geology, and biology.

The Perot Museum is also a great place to visit for families. The museum is designed to be both fun and educational, with a range of activities and exhibits that are suitable for visitors of all ages. Whether you're a parent looking to educate your children or a grandparent seeking a fun and engaging experience with your grandchildren, the Perot Museum has something for everyone.

In addition to its world-class exhibits and educational opportunities, the Perot Museum is also a beautiful and architecturally stunning building. The museum was designed by the world-renowned architect

Thom Mayne, and it features a unique and modern design that is both functional and aesthetically pleasing. Whether you're an architecture enthusiast or just looking for a beautiful place to spend the day, the Perot Museum is definitely worth a visit.

Finally, the Perot Museum is conveniently located in the heart of downtown Dallas, making it an easy and accessible destination for visitors. The museum is surrounded by several other attractions, including the Dallas Arboretum and Botanical Garden, the Dallas World Aquarium, and the AT&T Stadium, making it the perfect destination for a day trip or a weekend getaway.

In conclusion, the Perot Museum of Nature and Science is a world-class museum that offers a unique and engaging learning experience for visitors of all ages. With its state-of-the-art exhibits, commitment to science education, and beautiful architecture, the museum is a must-visit destination for anyone interested in exploring the wonders of science and the natural world. Whether you're a student, a scientist, or just looking for a fun and educational day out, the Perot Museum is the perfect destination for you.

8

Chapter 8

Klyde Warren Park

The Klyde Warren Park is a 5.2-acre urban park located in the heart of Dallas, Texas. It is a beautiful green oasis that provides a much-needed escape from the busy city life, and it is the perfect destination for anyone looking to relax, play, and enjoy the outdoors. If you're looking for a fun and beautiful place to spend the day, then the Klyde Warren Park is a must-visit destination.

One of the reasons why you should visit the Klyde Warren Park is its beautiful and well-manicured grounds. The park features lush lawns, beautiful gardens, and a variety of trees and shrubs, making it the perfect place to relax and enjoy the beautiful weather in Dallas. Whether you're looking to stretch out on the lawn, take a stroll through the gardens, or just sit and watch the world go by, the Klyde Warren Park has something for everyone.

Another reason to visit the Klyde Warren Park is its wide range of activities and events. The park is a hub of activity, with a variety of programs and events taking place throughout the year, including live music performances, food truck festivals, and outdoor yoga classes. Whether you're looking for a fun and interactive experience or just a peaceful and relaxing day out, the Klyde Warren Park has something for everyone.

The Klyde Warren Park is also a great destination for families. The park features a variety of play areas and activities for kids, including a children's park, a playground, and a splash pad. The park is also home to a variety of food trucks, cafes, and restaurants, making it the perfect place to grab a bite to eat with the family.

In addition to its beautiful grounds and exciting activities, the Klyde Warren Park is also a great place to visit for its location. The park is located in the heart of downtown Dallas, making it a convenient and accessible destination for visitors. The park is surrounded by several other popular attractions, including the AT&T Stadium, the Dallas World Aquarium, and the Perot Museum of Nature and Science, making it the perfect place to spend the day or a weekend getaway.

The Klyde Warren Park is also an environmentally-friendly destination. The park is designed to be sustainable and eco-friendly, with a variety of initiatives in place to reduce waste and conserve energy. From its use of rainwater harvesting to its extensive recycling programs, the Klyde Warren Park is a great example of how cities can create beautiful public spaces while also reducing their impact on the environment.

In conclusion, the Klyde Warren Park is a beautiful and vibrant urban park that offers something for everyone. With its well-manicured grounds, exciting activities and events, and eco-friendly initiatives, the park is a must-visit destination for anyone looking to escape the hustle and bustle of city life and enjoy the great outdoors. Whether you're a family, a couple, or just looking for a peaceful day out, the Klyde Warren Park is the perfect destination for you.

9

Chapter 9

The Dallas World Aquarium

The Dallas World Aquarium is a world-class facility located in the heart of Dallas, Texas. It is a place where visitors of all ages can immerse themselves in the wonders of the world's oceans and learn about the diverse and fascinating creatures that call these waters home. If you're looking for a fun, educational, and exciting experience, then the Dallas World Aquarium is a must-visit destination.

One of the reasons why you should visit the Dallas World Aquarium is its impressive collection of marine life. The aquarium is home to a wide range of species, including colorful fish, sea turtles, rays, and more. Visitors can observe these creatures up close in several large tanks and aquariums, including the massive Mayan jungle exhibit, which features a two-story glass tunnel where visitors can walk among the animals.

Another reason to visit the Dallas World Aquarium is its interactive exhibits and educational programs. The aquarium offers a variety of hands-on activities and exhibits, including touch tanks and interactive displays, that allow visitors to learn about the animals and their habitats in a fun and engaging way. The aquarium also offers a variety of educational programs, such as behind-the-scenes tours and animal encounters, that allow visitors to get an up-close and personal look at the animals and learn about the important role they play in our world.

The Dallas World Aquarium is also a great destination for families. The aquarium is designed with kids in mind, with a variety of interactive exhibits and hands-on activities that are perfect for children of all ages. From the interactive touch tanks to the animal encounters, there is something for kids of all ages to enjoy at the Dallas World Aquarium.

In addition to its impressive collection of marine life and interactive exhibits, the Dallas World Aquarium is also a great place to visit for its location. The aquarium is located in the heart of downtown Dallas, making it a convenient and accessible destination for visitors. The aquarium is surrounded by several other popular attractions, including the AT&T Stadium, the Klyde Warren Park, and the Perot Museum of Nature and Science, making it the perfect place to spend the day or a weekend getaway.

The Dallas World Aquarium is also a leader in conservation and animal welfare. The aquarium is committed to the care and well-being of the animals in its care and works to promote conservation efforts for species and their habitats. From its research programs to its conservation initiatives, the Dallas World Aquarium is making a difference in the world and helping to ensure that these amazing creatures will be around for generations to come.

In conclusion, the Dallas World Aquarium is a world-class facility that offers something for everyone. With its impressive collection of marine life, interactive exhibits, and commitment to conservation and animal welfare, the aquarium is a must-visit destination for anyone looking to immerse themselves in the wonders of the world's oceans and learn about the fascinating creatures that call these waters home. Whether you're a family, a couple, or just looking for a fun and educational experience, the Dallas World Aquarium is the perfect destination for you.

10

Chapter 10

Reunion Tower

Reunion Tower is a landmark skyscraper located in the heart of Dallas, Texas. It is a unique and iconic structure that offers visitors an unparalleled view of the city and its surrounding areas. If you're looking for a thrilling and unforgettable experience, then Reunion Tower is a must-visit destination.

One of the reasons why you should visit Reunion Tower is its 360-degree observation deck. The deck, which is located 470 feet above the ground, offers breathtaking views of the city and its surroundings. Visitors can see for miles in every direction and enjoy panoramic views of downtown Dallas, the surrounding countryside, and beyond. The observation deck is an ideal place for taking photos and creating memories that will last a lifetime.

Another reason to visit Reunion Tower is its interactive exhibits and multimedia displays. The tower offers a variety of interactive exhibits and displays that allow visitors to learn about the history of Dallas, its landmarks and attractions, and the surrounding area. The multimedia displays provide visitors with an immersive experience that highlights the city's rich history, culture, and diversity.

Reunion Tower is also a popular destination for families. The tower's interactive exhibits and multimedia displays are designed with kids in mind, making it a fun and educational experience for the whole family. Children will love exploring the exhibits and learning about the city and its surroundings, while adults will enjoy the breathtaking views from the observation deck.

In addition to its observation deck and interactive exhibits, Reunion Tower is also a great place to dine. The tower features a rotating restaurant, called Five Sixty by Wolfgang Puck, that offers a unique dining experience with breathtaking views of the city. The restaurant serves a variety of delicious dishes made with fresh ingredients, making it a perfect destination for a special occasion or a romantic evening out.

The location of Reunion Tower is another reason why you should visit. The tower is located in the heart of downtown Dallas, making it a convenient and accessible destination for visitors. It is surrounded by several other popular attractions, including the AT&T Stadium, the Klyde Warren Park, and the Perot Museum of Nature and Science, making it the perfect place to spend the day or a weekend getaway.

In conclusion, Reunion Tower is a landmark skyscraper that offers visitors an unforgettable experience. With its 360-degree observation deck, interactive exhibits, and multimedia displays, the tower is a must-visit destination for anyone looking to explore the city of Dallas and its surroundings. Whether you're a family, a couple, or just looking for a unique and thrilling experience, Reunion Tower is the perfect destination for you. So, go ahead, plan your trip to Reunion Tower and experience the beauty of Dallas from new heights.

11

Chapter 11

The Dallas Museum of Art

The Dallas Museum of Art is a world-renowned art museum located in the heart of Dallas, Texas. The museum boasts an impressive collection of over 24,000 works of art, including everything from ancient artifacts to contemporary masterpieces. If you're an art lover or simply interested in exploring the world of art and culture, then the Dallas Museum of Art is a must-visit destination.

One of the reasons why you should visit the Dallas Museum of Art is its extensive collection of art from around the world. The museum's collection includes works from ancient civilizations, such as Greece and Rome, as well as from regions like Africa, Asia, and Europe. Visitors can explore the galleries and admire masterpieces from some of the world's most renowned artists, such as Pablo Picasso, Vincent van Gogh, and Rembrandt.

Another reason to visit the Dallas Museum of Art is its commitment to education and community engagement. The museum offers a variety of programs and events for visitors of all ages, including art classes, workshops, and lectures. These programs are designed to help visitors of all ages and backgrounds gain a deeper appreciation and understanding of the art and the world around them.

The museum is also a popular destination for families. Children will love exploring the galleries and discovering the world of art, while adults will appreciate the museum's educational programs and the opportunity to admire some of the world's most impressive works of art. The museum is an excellent place to spend a family day out, and children under 12 are admitted for free.

The Dallas Museum of Art is also a great place to relax and unwind. The museum's beautiful gardens provide visitors with a peaceful escape from the hustle and bustle of the city. Visitors can take a stroll through the gardens and enjoy the beauty of nature while admiring the works of art on display.

In addition to its impressive collection and commitment to education, the Dallas Museum of Art is also a vibrant cultural center. The museum regularly hosts a variety of exhibitions and events that highlight the latest in contemporary art and culture. Visitors can enjoy exhibitions of works by local and international artists, attend concerts and performances, and take part in a variety of other cultural events.

The location of the Dallas Museum of Art is another reason why you should visit. The museum is located in the heart of Dallas, making it a convenient and accessible destination for visitors. It is surrounded by several other popular attractions, including the AT&T Stadium, the Klyde Warren Park, and the Perot Museum of Nature and Science, making it the perfect place to spend the day or a weekend getaway.

In conclusion, the Dallas Museum of Art is a world-renowned art museum that offers visitors an unforgettable experience. With its extensive collection, commitment to education, and vibrant cultural events, the museum is a must-visit destination for anyone looking to explore the world of art and culture. So, go ahead, plan your trip to the Dallas Museum of Art and immerse yourself in the beauty of art and culture.

12

Chapter 12

Bishop Arts District

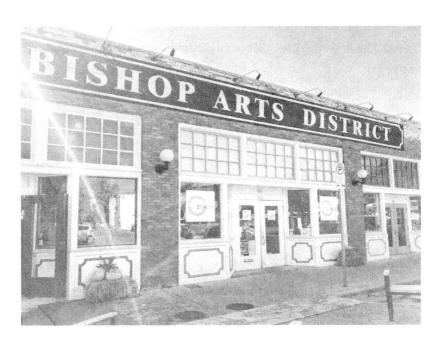

The Bishop Arts District in Dallas, Texas is a vibrant and thriving neighborhood that offers visitors a unique and memorable experience. Located just minutes from downtown Dallas, this eclectic and charming neighborhood is known for its charming streets, vibrant arts scene, and fantastic dining options. If you're looking for a fun and lively place to visit, the Bishop Arts District is the perfect destination.

One of the reasons why you should visit the Bishop Arts District is its thriving arts scene. The neighborhood is home to a variety of art galleries, theaters, and performance spaces that showcase the work of local artists and performers. Visitors can explore the galleries and enjoy a variety of exhibitions and performances, from contemporary art to live theater and music.

Another reason to visit the Bishop Arts District is its fantastic dining scene. The neighborhood is home to a variety of fantastic restaurants, cafes, and bars that offer a range of cuisine and drinks to suit every taste and budget. From gourmet cafes and farm-to-table restaurants to casual bars and pubs, visitors can find a delicious meal or drink to enjoy while they explore the neighborhood.

The Bishop Arts District is also a great place to shop and browse. The neighborhood is home to a variety of unique boutiques and shops that offer everything from handmade goods and vintage finds to artisanal foods and gifts. Visitors can spend hours browsing the shops and picking up unique items to take home with them.

The Bishop Arts District is also a popular destination for families. Children will love exploring the vibrant and colorful streets, visiting the art galleries, and trying out the various restaurants and cafes. The neighborhood is an excellent place to spend a family day out, and kids of all ages are sure to have a great time.

In addition to its vibrant arts and dining scenes, the Bishop Arts District is also a great place to relax and unwind. The neighborhood's charming streets and vibrant atmosphere provide visitors with a unique and lively escape from the hustle and bustle of the city. Visitors can take a leisurely stroll through the streets, enjoy a delicious meal or drink, and simply soak up the laid-back atmosphere of the neighborhood.

The location of the Bishop Arts District is another reason why you should visit. The neighborhood is located just minutes from downtown Dallas, making it a convenient and accessible destination for visitors. It is also close to several other popular attractions, including the Dallas Museum of Art, the AT&T Stadium, and the Perot Museum of Nature and Science, making it the perfect place to spend the day or a weekend getaway.

In conclusion, the Bishop Arts District is a vibrant and thriving neighborhood that offers visitors a unique and unforgettable experience. With its thriving arts scene, fantastic dining options, charming streets, and laid-back atmosphere, the neighborhood is a must-visit destination for anyone looking to explore the best of Dallas, Texas. So, go ahead, plan your trip to the Bishop Arts District and immerse yourself in the vibrant and eclectic culture of this charming neighborhood.

Printed in Great Britain
by Amazon